Destroying the Silence

Julie Campbell

Presentation by *BookLeaf Publishing*

Web: www.bookleafpub.com

E-mail: info@bookleafpub.com

ISBN: 9789358734140

First edition 2023

ACKNOWLEDGEMENT

Thank you Colin for supporting me through everything.

Slam

When my parents were still
married my brother and I
shared a room equipped
with blue walls and carpet.
We played in our empty closet
swinging our tiny bodies
where clothes belonged.

One day Kevin let go
of the metal bar urging
me to follow.
I trailed close behind
When I did he slammed
the door in my face
and on my four fingers
sitting in the door jamb.
He locked them tight.

I screamed my hand
paralyzed and throbbing
Kevin laughed behind
the closed door.
My mom met my scream
unlocking the door
faced with my spurting

blood like a fountain
my nails lost somewhere
in the blue.

She helped me to the kitchen.
I wailed as she put my tiny
hand under cold water.
The phone attached to her ear
desperately trying to reach our
doctor. She moved my father's
Banker's Club vodka from
the table. Sighing she
wrapped my hand in
a white towel to stop
the bleeding.

Orange Metal

My grandmother
always told me to brush
the hair out of my eyes.
She squealed: Everyone
wants to see your
beautiful face.
I crinkled my nose
like tomato juice
slithered up my nostrils.

I smuggled
the orange scissors
into my room. Four
fingers fit awkwardly
into large handles.
I brushed the long locks
into the front of my face.
Blond strands
tickled my chin.

I raised
the scissors to my forehead
the metal cold on my bare
skin creating goosebumps
across my scalp. I grasped

control taking a handful
of hair twisting it between
my middle and pointer finger
with a quick snip.
I let the hair fall to the blue
carpet. My new bangs sat
crooked on my forehead.
I grinned at the reflection
knowing it was all mine.

Opening a Salon

I never took good
care of my Barbies®.
I threw them around
letting their bodies
soar until they smacked
into a wall, shrieking
through their flight.

I grew rats' nest
until all of Barbies®
had afros. I tried to fix
them. I took my tiny
pink brush to the knots.
It only got stuck.
I could not let
Mom see the Barbie®
casualties.

There had to be
a solution to
fix their tangled dos
and avoid danger.
I closed my hands
through my favorite
orange handled scissors

cutting off the plastic
hair letting it gather
into a large bush.

Avoid, If You Can

In first grade I carried
a purple and pink lunchbox.
I never let Mom
wash it despite her pleas.
The last time
My mom packed
my lunch I unzipped
the box and flipped
open the lid. I inhaled
chunky sour milk leading me
to spew unidentifiable
chunks splashing the brown
table. Other kids clutched
their peanut butter and jelly
to their chest evading
my slop like they avoided
the metal slide on a hot day
not wanting to burn their thighs.
The monitor grabbed me by
the arm escorting me to the nurse
who promptly called my mother
who rushed from Allentown Business
School to my aid. On the way
home she snapped,
If you're not really sick

I'm going to be livid.
I shrunk in my seat
shunning her stare wishing I
had let her wash the box
the night before.

My Lucky Charm

At my Dad's company
picnic Kevin and I
wandered off on his boss'
large under-construction
property. We soon found
ourselves with the horses.
We watched awestruck
then climbed through
the fence. Kevin urged
me to run behind them
assuring me they liked to be
chased at ten I still believed him
When the horses came past
I scampered closely behind a black
horse. His horseshoe punched
me in the chest
launching me backward.
I landed in a ball and rolled down
the hill. My father was found
in a discreet corner. He snuffed out
his joint to confront the bright red
U pulsating on my chest.

Vodka on a Wednesday Night

i.
For the first ten years
I hated Wednesdays
the ugly plaid couch
the mock living room, where
I held my glass of water
in my left hand
it was still full.
It was always still full.
My father:
phone in one hand
the absolut lemon in the other
the bottle he loved more than his children.

ii.
I find myself coughing
my father asks, "Are you okay?"
I ignore him
like a class tunes out a teacher
giving a lecture
I bury my face
further in the plaid
breathing the smoky stench in
coughing again.
My father spins me over

knocking my water off the end table
spilling it everywhere
his white as cocaine Hanes
step in it as the
ignorant blue carpet absorbs it
my eyes stay zippered shut
the only feeling
I have
are his
five fingers
hitting
my face.

Redo

My mom met Jim
at Pizza Como.
She showed up
in baggy black sweats
with fading zombie
makeup on her face.
A year went by
until she introduced
us to him.

Kevin
irate still idolizing
our father. Not
yet knowing the dangers
of that worship.

Me
following Kevin
I also pushed Jim away
instead I wanted
a family.
Just the three of us.

Four years later
they were married

We grew into Jim
hoped a family
would emerge
in the end.
Kevin and I grinned
to each other
thinking this was our
redo.
Fourteen years later
she would leave him.

Pigtails

Kevin hung with
the "in" crowd
Older boys
that pulled out their cigarettes
at the bus stop.
Being thirteen
months younger
I like to follow
Kevin and those boys.

The last time
I took the walk
with Kevin
up the steep hill
to the apartment building,
my hair was crookedly
parted and pulled
into long pigtails.
We reached the boys
riding their bikes
in the street
ignoring the cars.

The fattest boy
wiped the sweat

perpetuating from his
brow with a meaty arm.
He smirked my way
remarking,
Hey look guys,
Kevin brought
us a blowjob
with handlebars.

Robbery

I.
Jim had a pair of orange-handled
scissors. He left them in the living room
handles facing out of a white box with
gold trimming. When he went to bed
I took them in my room cutting paper
stars and snowflakes. The next day
I snuck them back into the box
before Jim noticed they were gone.

II.
In seventh grade my teacher made us
do an activity. He put out supplies
including half-dried-out markers,
two pairs of orange-handled scissors,
and numerous amounts of crappy
rusted metal righty and lefty scissors,
that never cut. I pounced on the
orange scissors cutting along
the dotted edges with precision.
At the end of class I put the
scissors in my backpack. At home
I scratched off the name Mr. Korceinski
and wrote my own in black marker.

Standing at the Top

I was ten years
old when
we stood tall
above our hill.
Breathing deep,
sucking in the dry
wintry air,
until my brother
took the leap.

You ran so fast
and tumbled
down our hill.
We laughed fluently
when your body
collapsed
against the frost-bitten
grass-less hill.

I can still
hear our cackles
echo.

Keeping Time

I watched you pound the stick
against the snare.
I always loved the drums.
I tried to play them once,
unlike you I could only
succeed on Rockband. You understood
the notes, I could only
comprehend colors—red, green, blue, yellow
occasionally an orange.

At fourteen my breath
thrummed against yours,
while cats argued under my neighbors
porch. You leaned in close
our lips touched like you tapped
the bass for a pause.

While you thrashed
on the drums I picked up a guitar.
You could smack a snare
and I could finger the frets.

Orange Metal II

I didn't brush my hair
in middle school.
It grew to the
middle of my back
but I never let the
bristles through my locks.

Mom nagged me to let her
twist the strands together
into a French braid.
I ducked her advances
not wanting her yanking
at my scalp. I pictured
blood spots forming
where she jerked the hair from
my head.

Instead I took my new scissors,
isolated the rat's nest growing
in the back of my head. I pinned the
detangled hair on top of my skull
leaving the knotty bush hanging
from my scalp. One clean snip
let the bush roll like a tumbleweed
down my back.

When my mom asked to braid
my hair. I let her. I had rid
myself of the knot on my own.
As she entwined pieces of my hair
together she discovered the chopped
chunk. Chuckling she called our hairdresser
assuring me I'd prefer it short, anyway.

Swerve

I still don't know how I made it home.
Kevin wasn't there to steer for you
leaving me to stare at the empty bottle
on the floor of the passenger seat.
You grab my leg, squeeze hard,
and ask if I love you slurring your words.

I wrench my leg away ignoring the words
imagining jumping from the car running home.
I clench my teeth together as you
swerve across the yellow lines the bottle
of Banker's bouncing onto my seat.
You bring us back to our side with a hard

turn of the wheel. My knees knock hard
against each other. I want to screech angry
words.
You pull up to my house I loosely hug you and
run home.
I imagine you driving back to Kevin you
tightly clutch the Banker's vodka bottle
in your hand then toss it into my old seat.

Once inside I take a seat
in a gray recliner. I close my eyes hard.

The phone rings and your words
greet me again asking for Mom. She's home
and puts the receiver to her ear. You
change her plans she knows your bottle

is empty. She yells for Jim hoping he can bottle
his jealousy and they leave me in my seat
to rescue Kevin from Dad's hard
fist. Jim took a metal bat to use over words
and hurt you the way you hurt us. I stay home
wanting, wishing I could watch you

squirm under Mom's words. Instead you
try to walk on your porch with a new bottle
in hand. Kevin runs out takes a seat
away from you. Your steps stomp hard
on the porch. Jim swings the bat tries words
to entice, Come off your porch mother fucker.
Your home

is the deck. Their words can't make you leave
home.
Stumbling falling hard to the wood, you
pull yourself into a seat searching for a bottle.

Swerve II

D:
Kevin and I are with you
I sit in the back of your
mini-van my seat belt unbuckled.
You bang your hand against
the dashboard demanding
Kevin hit the ball not strike out.
He flinches away from your
fist flattening his hand against
the window. I watch hands fall
from the wheel as your head flops
against the seat. Kevin attempts
to reach the steering wheel
and fails. We swerve over
the grass into oncoming traffic
Kevin crouches underneath
the dashboard I pull my knees
to my chest while tears fall
against my kneecaps.
I feel the impact
I hear the metal crunch
together into an accordion
and the screams of the
elderly couple you killed.
 I black-out.

R:
Nobody will tell us
what happened to you.
Jim slides the article
into Mom's hands.
She sends the piece
our way Kevin and I
stare at each other dumbstruck
waiting for a phone call
that never seems to come.
I'm still not sure
what you did.
I've transferred some
of my own details to
the story you refuse
to tell us.

Our Feeble Noose

This is not going to make you happy.
I sat underneath the Bethlehem Star
to plunder underneath your words
reaching through the clutter
rifling between what pierces and ignites.
I am not going to take the blame
for what you tried to do.

The rope's cutting off circulation.
My thoughts begin to hinder my speech
I've lost my way through our unwanted
mess. I've tried to reel us in, but I am sucked
dry by this leech you've attached to my brain.
I feel my heart clench and tremble
I can't unknot the rope this time.

Snow Fall in Arrowhead

Today we didn't need
our tubes to fly
down.
We tried to run up
the icy hill
instead our feet
fumbled underneath us.
We made it halfway
then skated
to the bottom.

We looked up at
the hill behind
the clubhouse.
Brother and sister:
remembering the treacherous
slope, our family
standing below us
waiting to snap
a picture
of our faces
grinning, giddy
from the descent.

Inmate: GA6910

I didn't go for you.
Grandma cried at dinner
when I rejected your calls.
So I let them drive me to
Camp Hill.
Kevin still refused.
He didn't want to see
you that way.
I couldn't care less.
We stood in line
waiting to check in
with your inmate
number.

Your number was called
and we stood in another line.
I held my hands out
while a clothed wand
searched for drugs on
my palms. Next
I beeped and removed
my belt. I still beeped
and had to pull my
underwire metal bra
from my chest. I bounced

through beep less.

We walked in a white
corridor then into
a crowded room
adorned with upright
blue chairs connected
with a metal bar. You stood
by a large desk in the middle
of the room wearing a
brown jumpsuit
with the words
INMATE
stamped on your back
in white lettering.

You leaned over
to hug me. You
lingered and whispered
thank you. The spicy
tomato juice on your
breath slithered up
my nose that
crinkled like it always
does when you talk.

Up All Night

You said you snorted
white powder
and stayed
up all night.

You would come home
    wired
incapable of coherence.

You pretended
to sleep until you knew
you could get
                out.

You snuck
back in at four in the
morning, darkness still
settled around your house,
everyone else's eyes
smeared with sleep
yours were swollen
    bloodshot.

You said you slept
for days once

the white powder
wore off.

You said you wanted
me to learn from your
mistakes
          not repeat them.

Elevation Escape

Jim's
son Jamie
and I walked
across rocks and
eventually began hiking
up a mountain. We didn't
mean to. Our walk just started
going uphill. We climbed over fallen
logs and kept stability when rocks slipped
from underneath our feet. Soon enough we
found
the top. Jamie ducked into an opening with rocks
enclosing
us. We sat on the cold rocks and he pulled a blue
glass pipe from
his pocket and a small zip-lock bag. He
sprinkled the green into the
bowl then tossed the black lighter to my corner
and I lit up. Smoke
engulfed me. We passed it between each other
filling up our lungs and our
small enclosure with clouds. A hawk swooped
over our heads. We watched through

the small crevice of our solitude. We giggled at
an altitude higher than I ever thought I would
get.

Just Before Dinner

It was a quick push.
My feet dangled
over the balcony
I sat high
while you wanted
to shove me
　　　　　　　down.

You let your children
sit upon the ledge
you built them a pedestal
all the while knocking me
　　　　　　　　down.

I felt your hand
firmly press
into my back
arching my spine
lurching to the gritty
　　　　　　　ground.

I landed cat-like:
knees in muddy soil,
my hands dripping
with resentment.

I pushed to my feet
and ran once they hit

                    ground.

Soccer Field Sweetheart

We drove to Lehigh
soccer fields and parked
his maroon Jeep in the middle of
the field. I climbed into
the back. We had plenty of space
with the seats pushed down.
We giggled fumbling with
our clothes. I leaned my hips
into his while he pulled
the jeans from my body.
We entangled our bodies
together enclosed under
the roof of his car.
I traced my pointer finger
along the fogged window
Colin helped me clasp my bra
he smiled at the heart
in the corner of his windshield
and wiped the sweat
from his forehead.